CONTEMPRICKS

Contemporary Issues. Limerick Hues.

Rabbali 'Ihaka'

Qurate
quratebooks.com

CONTEMPRICKS

Rabbali 'Ihaka'

Published in 2024

© Published by

Qurate
qauratebooks.com

Qurate Books Pvt. Ltd.
Goa 403523, India
www.quratebooks.com
Tel: 1800-210-6527, Email: info@quratebooks.com

ISBN: 9789358986747

WRITER's NOTE

'CONTEMPRICKS' Explained

As mentioned in the tag line, it is:

CONTEMP*orary Issues. Lime***RICK** *Hues.*

To understand better, a Limerick is a 5-liner fun-filled poetry. The humour can be both simple and slightly tongue-in-cheek!

Limerick follows a rhyming pattern of aabba.

I too have adopted this format or meter but taken some liberties with the fun-filled genre, bringing in other emotions of pathos, pensive thoughts, advice, suggestions, and even food-for-thought! But never with the intent of hurting anyone – the foremost principle has been: No Hurt, Just Skirt i.e. simply skirting or bringing forth different viewpoints, without any intention of hurting.

WHY these CONTEMPRICKS?

Though, these are meant for everyone, in their mid-teens and above; these are particularly targeted towards GEN Z (born roughly between mid-1990s and 2010) or GEN α (Alpha, born roughly between 2010 and 2024), and going into the future, GEN β (Beta, from 2024 onwards)……

Why so?

Owing to the fast life, multi-tasking at work and/or home, plethora of social handles to keep abreast with, information bombardment from social media; Gen Z and onwards are forever looking for time-saving methods – they are usually at home with

- bullet points,
- multiple, single-phrase sentences for WhatsApp messaging,
- short reels,

- concise tweets and blogs,
- and the like.

In such an environment, I have come up with these 5-racy liners on each topic i.e. Contemporary Topics - Limerick Optics, which tries to explain various subjects conceptually, in what I term the 'REACH' methodology viz. Rhythmically, Educationally, Analytically, Comprehensively, and Holistically – you can take my word that each CONTEMPRICK will not take more than 30 seconds, and that is the beauty of the crispy KISS (keeping it short & simple) CONTEMPRICKS!

Some examples are:

Eco-Balancing (Theme 1, § 5),

Heat Index (Theme 1, § 12),

Party Hopping (Theme 2, § 9),

Mini Vote/Referendum (Theme 2, § 11),

Democracy Forms (Theme 2, § 20),

MSP (Theme 2, § 21),

India – Parliamentary Democracy (Theme 2, § 25),

Power Equation (Theme 2, § 29),

USA Constitution (Theme 3, § 6),

Religio-Politico Mix (Theme 4, § 3),

Most of the Contempricks in Theme 5, and

Many Contempricks in Theme 9

I have intentionally and thoughtfully categorised these CONTEMPRICKS broadly under 9 Themes viz.

- Environment/Climate change related
- Healthy Critiquing on different issues
- International incidents
- (A)political activities
- Festivals (both religious and others) and their raison d'etre
- Fragmentation of polity

- Sports and Entertainment focussed
- Judicial rulings (having far-reaching repercussions)
- Philosophical interpretation

which means that there is a wholesome bouquet for everyone, with each topic under these thematic sections, encapsulated in just 5-quick lines! These take about 10 seconds to read, and say, another 20 seconds to understand/internalise/digest, especially those which are a little more profound in content.

Since these are on aspects which are contemporary, a brief context and approximate occurrence period is also mentioned at the end of each CONTEMPRICK, in italicised parentheses, for better appreciation by the reader.

Sit back, Relax and Enjoy!

Rabbali 'Ihaka'

WHAT'S IN A NAME?!

RABBALI 'IHAKA'

Rabbali: The conjunction, and need I dare say, confluence of Rabba and Ali – the pious and pristine names of The Almighty!

'Ihaka': This is a very powerful and meaningful Maori word – Maoris are the original inhabitants of possibly the world's best place New Zealand (besides one's owncountry/ motherland)!

'Ihaka' is my 'takhallus' i.e. pen-name.

'Ihaka' means 'A Blunt Instrument'.

One meaning of 'blunt' is 'not sharp', as in 'a blunt knife'.

'Blunt' has also another usage, as in 'he is very blunt' i.e. frank -

Frankness that can be piercingly 'sharp', at times!

So, 'Ihaka' is a very interesting dichotomous word with two meanings and both are 'antonyms' i.e. 'not sharp' and 'sharp'!

This is the etymology of my creative name, Rabbali 'Ihaka'.

ACKNOWLEDGEMENTS

I dedicate this book to LIFE itself! 'Cos, life is the greatest teacher!

At the outset, I would like to thank my wife and my children, who have taught me immensely, be it through their love (or hate), sacrifice (or demands), adulation (or despise), understanding (or misunderstanding), support (or otherwise)!

Though, I thank The Creator, I have not seen Him/Her (except, maybe, in dreams) but the gods, I have seen have been our parents and parent-like elders, in my life, whom I would like to thank for my upbringing. What I am has been moulded by their values instilled in me – with them also, I have experienced and learned from the same dichotomous emotions of love, anger, et al.....

{The above two i.e. me and my children, and me and my parents, I feel, is a generational gap issue, wherein the newer/younger/generation-next is more impatient than the previous, primarily because of the changing environment and corresponding value systems, e.g. if newspaper was an 'essential', in our times, for contemporary news; today, with the numerous social media platforms, on which there is a 24x7 bombardment of news and information, it renders the 'daily' virtually redundant for Gen Z!

The daily chore of waiting for the newspaper's delivery to smelling the newsprint to thumbing its flying, unstitched pages, glued over it with a cuppa coffee or tea, mulling over the articles and editorials for the better part of an hour, gave us a sense of satisfaction, which is possibly a 'time-waste' for Gen Z, in their fast-paced, short eye-span life. Possibly, blogs and tweets satiate them with the 'other' view, which our generation finds difficult to comprehend – and this is the kind of generational change, I have alluded to.}

I would be greatly failing, if I did not acknowledge my teachers, who were equally responsible in shaping and sharpening my mental faculties, from a very young stage in life.

And both my relatives and friends (& foes), who knowingly or unknowingly helped me in my journey of trying to understand and overcome the challenges of this world and its people!

There have been some chance or short-lived acquaintances too or people from whom I faced rejection/opposition but who too influenced and gave maturity & strength to my thinking -- so, I thank them too, from the depth of my heart!

Last but not the least, I thank all those, including Indian Authors Academy, Qurate, who have motivated and supported me in bringing this book to life!

God Bless everyone!

Rabbali 'Ihaka'

TABLE OF CONTENTS

THEME 1

ENVIRONMENTALLY ENLIGHTENED

§ 1. HEAVY RAINS IN GUJARAT

Do not have weather jitters
Enjoy the rains and the fritters
Start preparing for the garba spree
Stay cool with a cuppa hot coffee/tea
Or merry and safe even with some bitters

[Context: Unusual timing, Unprecedented rains in Gujarat - mid Sep '23]

§ 2. POLLUTION POLITICS

P for Politics and Pollution - People dying but
politics continues even over pollution

Unchecked growth, Winds, Fossil power, GE crop cycle,
Stubble burn, Vehicles are all part of the equation

Centre blames State, and State blames
neighbouring States - new controversies are born

State powers into one neighbour, finger pointing
changes to others - but life just goes on

Blame game, experimental measures - 'tis poor
governance: decibalised drama sans solution

[Context: Delhi's perennial pollution at the onset of winters - end Nov '23]

§ 3. CLIMATE CHANGE

Climate is changing, the world over, like nothing before
Unscheduled rains, snow, tempest, quakes and many such more
Mother Nature's fury, wrath and ire seems to be on fire
Many more things besides farmers' planting and harvesting are in straits dire
Introspect - Man's own greed, wasteful callousness is at the very core

[Context: Negative climatic changes due to man's greed - early Dec '23]

§ 4. 'GREEN' ENERGY

Harnessing of natural energy of sun, wind et al is paramount
Investing in such renewable sources of energy will make every penny count
Cop out should not be an option in discussions like COP28
Thankfully commonality was arrived at, for fossil fuel usage to abate
In years future, more energy will be put, in making 'green' energy, a fount

[Context: COP28 Event - mid Dec '23]

§ 5. ECO-BALANCING

After vehicles powered by petrol, diesel and CNG, EV
is the flavour of the season

Not only depleting, polluting carbons; mining lithium,
cobalt too is an eco-treason

Renewable, non-polluting energy sources need to be searcheth

With sea levels rising, Hydrogen from water holds
the best promise, ole' man Rabbali sayeth

For Hope of a better future world, Belief of
sustainability is a strong reason

[Context: Own perception of best option for vehicles' energy source - end Dec '23]

§ 6. THEN AND NOW

Winter's comforting sunshine used to follow pure mist and fog

Nowadays, curtained sun comes after a lazy, hazy smog

Summery nights were cool, sky-canvassing the milky way

Reckless industrialisation brought hot nights with a dusty spray

Balancing progress with yesteryears' picture perfect,
keeps the mind active and agog

[Context: Delhi's hazy, pollution crazy winters - mid Jan '24]

§ 7. BEAUTIFUL BALI

An escape to Bali can also be termed Baliscape
Where one is able to inhale and savour Bali's pristine landscape
Baliscape also represents the canvas of all things artistic & beautiful
Like the serene and green of Bali, and the ocean cool
For visitors, Bali is not an island but a Heavenly Cape

[Context: Namesake Paradise on Earth! - early Feb '24]

§ 8. CYCLICAL CHANGES

Winter rains have now arrived in Delhi, on 31st January
Bringing another cold wave, way after the usual day, Lohri
Weather is changing the world over
'Greenhouse' effect is showing its true colour
Farming timing and planning is all awry, not hunky dory

[Context: Unscheduled rains in Delhi - early Feb '24]

§ 9. LIVING THINGS' 'BALANCING ACT'

Ancient belief: Living things consist of
humans, animals and even trees

Total number is finite - when one increases,
the others decrease

As human population grows, animals
get extinct, deforestation occurs

More mouths/hunting/land's required - farm
productivity is upped but quality suffers

Flora: organic nutrients down; Humans:
sperm count down, with disease

[Context: Own philosophy - Equilibrium balancing of fixed number living things - end Mar '24]

§ 10. CLIMATIC RAINS IN GCC

Unprecedented rains in most of the GCC, Gulf Council Countries

Quirk of nature or cloud seeding, in the
desert countries, surrounded by jetties?

Most in the 75 years of met. recorded history,
UAE gets 255mm of rains

Dubai becomes 'Doob'ai (flooded), a very sorry sight
that clutches the hearts and pains

Can anyone fathom, unravel, control
Mother Nature and its mysteries?

[Context: Middle-east deserts inundated with torrential rains - mid Apr '24]

§ 11. EARTH DAY SIGNIFICANCE

Earth Day on 22nd April is celebrated to
save our planet's depleting health

Started by Sen. Gaylord Nelson in 1970, after
Santa Barbara's oil spill stealth

Each year, there is focus on one climate
change, ecological, environmental element or theme

Like this year, in more than 193 countries,
'Planet Vs Plastics' was the crying scream

For Preservation, Conservation and Sustainability; Govts.,
Corporates reserve, commit and utilise their wealth

[Context: Significance of Earth Day 2024 - 22042024]

§ 12. HEAT INDEX

Weather temperature has traditionally been
measured in degrees Fahrenheit or Celsius

New concepts, like winter's Chill Factor and
summer's Heat Index seem more real and conscious

Whilst Chill factor accounts for icy winds, Heat Index
takes humidity into consideration

In high temperatures, if humidity is high, the 'feel'
on the body is a bigger consternation

Then, even 47°C would seem like 56°C, as per Heat Index,
warning all to be extremely cautious

[Context: Met. Deptt.'s new heat 'feel' analysis - higher than the temperature - end May '24]

§ 13. CARLSBERG RIDGE RICHNESS

Carlsberg is not only famous for the frothy drink Atop but also
a ridge Underwater in northwestern Indian Ocean

It is a tectonic plate boundary formed 30 million years ago
at 1800m-3600m depth, but still under seismic activation

Seawater reacts with earth's inner crust spewing out
mineral rich lava, called magma

Sulphides of Zinc, Cobalt, Copper, Manganese, Silver, Gold,
Platinum, Rare Earths get deposited on sea terra firma

India is in the race to power pollution-free vehicles with
these rare-earth minerals upon excavation

[Context: India's foray into excavating the sea-bed - end May '24]

THEME 2

CRITIQUE-ALLY COUNTERED

§ 1. COUNTRY'S NAME

Bharat, India, Hindustan or Hindostan - all names
of our great nation

Symbolise different eras conjuring up history and passion

Common man has equal reverence

Both sides create needless reference

He wants better livelihood, not needless
name change diversion

[Context: Sudden anathema to the name India, usage of Bharat instead, on opposition acronym-ing its bloc INDIA - end Oct '23]

§ 2. SARDAR

A child born on 31st Oct, titled Sardar Patel, who united India

On 31st Oct, a sardar spitefully shot dead
India's 1st woman PM, Indira

Respect for Sardar and Sikhs remains - is it a Day
of Unity or Hatred?

Such like confabulations fill the mind, so sacred

Some with pride and some with conundrums
and melancholia

[Context: Significance of 31st Oct - end Oct '23]

§ 3. TWO-WAY DIALOGUE

In a meaningful democracy, dialogue has to be
an ongoing process

Only then the leader knows the public, and
junta has leader's mind's access

One way communication is like a
diktat, instruction and edict

Press conferences, debates, free
responsible media bestow some benefit

Otherwise only debaters, actors would form the ruling nexus

*[Context: Importance of 2-way dialogue Vs only one way
interaction - early Nov '23]*

§ 4. UTTARKASHI TUNNEL DISASTER

Another disaster, another success, kudos to our countrymen

In the frenetic pace to progress, forgotten was the how and when

Safety was given short shrift, while
escape routes were given the go-by

Victory shouts were made to drown
shortcomings and the reasons why

Unquestioned, Unfettered development is
too high a price for the lives of our brethren

[Context: Tragedy at the ill-fated, ill-designed Uttarkashi Tunnel - end Nov '23]

§ 5. POLL TYPES

Polls are numerous - Gallup, Pre-vote, Exit and the Counted

Mr Gallup's Opinion poll was amongst the first to be touted

Pre-vote and Exit may only show trends due to
many nuances and hues

Since people are generally discreet, shy and
reticent in sharing their views

The Final, Counted ones may also be rigged but
are the most sorted

[Context: Value of different types of polls - early Dec '23]

§ 6. GOVERNANCE

No system is 100% fool proof in providing governance to a country

This is what we have seen and experienced in
contemporary world history

While dictatorship fetters freedom, becomes
increasingly autocratic

Hung mandate, majoritarian intolerance
are a bane when it is too democratic

Benign dictatorship/monarchy is ideal but
very rare, and remains a wishful mystery

*[Context: Philosophising on which type of national governance
is better - end Dec '23]*

§ 7. COVERTLY OVERT

Suspension is from one side, Suspense from the other
Covert has become Overt, Loose words are rife - does it not bother?
Absolute numbers, unbridled power is democracy's undoing
Inability to clarify, tackle real issues - both sides of the divide are found wanting
Emotionally fooled, only vox populi is to be blamed for this huge mandate disaster

[Context: Huge election mandate Vs Other mandates; and their negative fallouts - end Dec '23]

§ 8. POLITICAL LANGUAGE

Political language is becoming crass, from the class decorum earlier
In India too, it has gone many notches down the tier
All sides are equally to blame, who started it is not the point
Slang and slander are messy but sadly make it massy and buoyant
Speeches have colloquial abuse, finesse of scripting is on the bier

[Context: Political language, etiquettes going to the grave - early Jan '24]

§ 9. PARTY HOPPING

When an elected rep. switches party allegiance mid-way
S/he brings a lot of discomfiture, disturbance, dismay
New Act to curb this 'aaya ram gaya ram' menace
needs promulgation
S/he cannot leave and other parties
cannot admit till next election
As free choice, if s/he still quits, s/he should remain
a representative sans benefits & pay

[Context: New Anti-Defection Law needed to curb party hopping with gay abandon e.g. MP, Maharashtra - early Jan '24]

§ 10. TRAFFIC WOES

Lo behold! In India, traffic woes are increasing
manifold, in cities, small/big, day by day
With flyovers on the increase, easy access
restricted, driving wrong side, is becoming 'my way'
Earlier only non-motorised vehicles were the offending culprits
Now, two and even four-wheeler motors are
charting out these circuits
Police's nonchalance; motorists don't navigate,
only manoeuvre opposing sways - a la walking jay

[Context: Traffic civic sense hits dust due to ill-planning and lack of fear of being monitored and caught - early Jan '24]

§ 11. MINI VOTE/REFERENDUM

On important issues, there should be a mini vote, a referendum
Each rep., in his area should obtain a mandate, an outcome
For normal important matters, there could be a simple franchise solidarity
But National, Constitutional issues should require minimum 2/3rds majority
Only then the ruling powers should action after getting the up thumb

[Context: Need, Value and SOP for Referendums - early Jan '24]

§ 12. SPACE VENTURING

Chandrayan, Mangalyan and Aditya space odysseys
By ISRO and scientists, have met with incredible successes
Huge accolades for what the teams have achieved
Wouldn't be possible if ISRO and IITs hadn't been conceived
And encouraged by today's leaders and initiating visionaries

[Context: Space Adventures & Successes, like Chandrayan, are due to early foundations laid - mid Jan '24]

§ 13. LIES AND FAKES - NEW HEADACHE

Lies and White lies, and now Fake and Deep fake
Both are concocted untruths, be wary, for Heaven's sake
Different eras conjure up different lingo and popular phrases
Language churning happens both in a continuum and phases
You pick your preference, a choco frappe or a choco shake

[Context: New-Age Deceiving Technology - mid Jan '24]

§ 14. GLIB TONGUE

Political Leaders are 'supposed' to do social re-engineering
Religious Gurus are 'supposed' to enlighten
spiritual understanding
'Supposed to' is the one which 'posed' this question
Extremely rare are leaders and gurus with
selfless, do-good intention
Nowadays, these good orators divide society
and minds, only for self-trumpeting

[Context: Religious events like Ayodhya Temple should be heralded by religious gurus, not political leaders - end Jan '24]

§ 15. EGOISM & EGOTISM

Chest size declaration or personal name guarantee is not humility

Half-sleeves Tee in winters, prompt people to think
of exuberant publicity

Ungrateful is, not acknowledging that today's success
is only possible due to seven decades of foundation

Unmindful is, not appreciating any good work done
in last decade's administration

Being ungrateful is a greater evil whereby egoism and
egotism is an absolute certainty

*[Context: Continuous Egoism & Egotism does not give
long-term success – end Jan '24]*

§ 16. FAKING SELF-DEATH

Is it creating awareness or cheap publicity,
When own death by cancer is faked, in the city?
Be it awareness of an ailment, disease, syndrome or illness
By spreading such false news, it only reeks of casualness
Which has propensity to garner ire, not sympathy

*[Context: Cheap publicity, like faking death, resorted to by
both commoners and leaders - early Feb '24]*

§ 17. PROGRESS, A CONTINUUM

Last decade's GDP growth was undoubtedly good
But many other parameters were not, as they should
Take-off was facilitated as base was firm and enabling
Strong foundation is a must for a beautiful, robust building
Progress is a continuum; credit is not only under one's own hood

[Context: Progress needs continuity, but cannot be achieved without an initial strong foundation - early Feb '24]

§ 18. UCC (UNIFORM CIVIL CODE)

Though UCC (Uniform Civil Code) for India is good in many aspects
Due to diversity, it needs to be broad-based in its sub-texts
But when different states of the Union start framing their own
Uniformity will be sacrificed surely, unbeknown
Exemptions, like for tribals, may lead to other similar religious pretexts

[Context: Different States, like Uttarakhand, implementing own UCC with own exemptions, seems to negate the concept - early Feb '24]

§ 19. SHIFTING EDITORIALS

Centrespreads have of late seen a shift due to sheer economics

Not talking of the glitzy magazines but of most dailies basic mix

Editorials and columns are relegated to the
end whilst centrefolds hold advertisements

Through which high revenue 'moolah' is raked in,
in mega bucks, not measly cents

Is the shift also metaphorical, indicative of loss of
specific punch and harping generics?

[Context: Daily Newspapers Editorials, no more Centrespreads - early Feb '24]

§ 20. DEMOCRACY FORMS

Democracy - both Presidential and Parliamentary, should
absorb from each other

Slightly longer term and maximum tenure of the
leader should be the change order

One President's tenure of max 2 terms should be
each of 5 years to get more work done

Similarly, one Prime Minister should be at the helm for
a max of 10 years to let new blood run

Old, bumbling leaders: a strict No; but advice from
them is welcome, should be no bother

*[Context: Parliamentary and Presidential Democracy should learn,
feed from each other - mid Feb '24]*

§ 21. MSP (MINIMUM SUPPORT PRICE)

MSP is a complex issue but should be ExCom (Executive Committee)
monitored and mandated

Foremost is cost calculation which should be country averaged
after being production quantum weighted

ExCom of 9 to be on similar lines of Arbitration Forum - 3 reps. each
of farmers and govt., 1 agri expert from each side, and 1 apex agri
expert selected by the two agri experts

MSP with X% profit should be adhered to but profits may be
discounted by farmer/s, if produce wastage hurts

ExCom to fix export percentage based on national food safety
net; and soil nutrition+water table to be the
basis for, which crops to be rotated

[Context: The raging MSP debate - mid Feb '24]

§ 22. GUILT-LESS GUILE

World over, in politics and politicians today, there is no
modicum of shame, pun unintended

Ad-bombing, viral media, (possibly 'deep fakes', in future) - people
are confused, with gossip/news inundated

Tall promises have been replaced by White lies

Bragging has become passe when Egotism flies

No semblance of guilt on feeding such misinfo - prevarication,
whataboutery, they feel vindicated

[Context: Today's politics of Fakes, Lies and Whataboutery - end Feb '24]

§ 23. SHAMEFUL VOTE BANK POLITICS

Fear from no one, Freedom to do anything, fosters Mafia Fiefdom

Where heinous loot of the body(rape) and soul(minerals/wild life) takes place, protected by the 'Powers' who succumb,

To vote bank politics, letting dastardly crimes thrive and penetrate

Inhumanly subjugating the entire area, letting atmosphere vitiate

Facilitating criminals' escape, for money and an electoral 'victory' outcome

[Context: Mafia-Political Nexus in illegal mining (e.g. Goa, Chhattisgarh, Rajasthan/Haryana) and rape - end Feb '24]

§ 24. SKELETONS IN THE CUPBOARD

All politicians across the world and spectrum have some skeletons in their cupboard

Show of money or position, Fear of agencies like I-T, ED.... is enough to get the opposition lured

The ruling party has always the greatest to offer

As it has many positions and shitload of funds in its coffer

No ethics/morals, zero conscience; and ideologies, loyalty, commitment are also blurred

[Context: Scruple less politics - when use of Govt agencies became apparent - end Feb '24]

§ 25. INDIA - PARLIAMENTARY DEMOCRACY

India, a sub-continent, with such diversity, should
remain a Parliamentary democracy

In many countries, Presidential form has shaped
up as a megalomaniac autocracy

Why re-invent when other sub-continent countries tried and failed?

Pakistan, Sri Lanka, Bangladesh changed to Presidential
polity and later recoiled

Proportional representation, maybe Yes, but Presidential form
has trappings of creating 'narcisscracy'

[Context: When debate for Presidential Form of Democracy for India re-surfaced - early Mar '24]

§ 26. PSYCHO ACTION

Any person, world over, who murders innocent children

Seems to be having brain chemical 'locha' boiling in a cauldron

They are mentally weak, confused and psychopaths

Requiring deep study on societal fabric, by sociopaths

The greatest tragedy is when such people are free, on the run

[Context: Individuals and Countries' (Israel-Hamas/Palestinian conflict) sick actions - end Mar '24]

§ 27. ELECTION SEASON

With the announcement of election dates
Gloves are out, election fever and frenzy open up all gates
Manifestos and tall promises become the order of the day
With unusual politeness, hectic campaigning by candidates in the fray
Creating new political equations, friends to foes or opposers becoming mates

[Context: Five yearly, World's largest election exercise rolls out - end Mar '24]

§ 28. TONGUE-IN-CHEEK

Double entendre, in public domain, should be within limits, even if very witty
Flying off the 'handle' while tweeting or posting on social media, reeks of insensitivity
In parliament, Churchill and our Piloo Mody were famous for their quips and wisecracks
Birbal and Ghalib too were credited with their one liner repartees and masked 'smacks'
Hitting below the belt, in private, may be fine but in the 'marketplace', it may become quite shitty

[Context: Supriya Shrinate's 'hacked' tweet on 'Mandi' going viral - end Mar '24]

§ 29. POWER EQUATION

How is 'Power' derived? - Hierarchy,
Constitution, Abdication or Snatching

The first two have an air of freedom, while the
last two are asphyxiating

At the zenith of mismanagement or tyranny, generally,
as seen around, military takes over

And in some other countries, religious fundamentalists
whip up emotions and usurp power

Warning: damning some of the unbridled
authority, judiciary is being forced to be uprising!!

[Context: SC passes strident anti-establishment judgements (Electoral Bonds, Mayoral polls - end Mar '24]

§ 30. 'SPINAL' BUREAUCRACY

In all countries, bureaucracies, for good or bad, run governments

In lax democracies they may be pen-pushers, whilst in
strong leadership countries, meek servants

Few are audacious enough to go against the grain

Whilst most others may frustrate and work for personal gain

But they remain the key to implementation and attainments

[Context: Political diktats vis-a-vis bureaucracy, for continuity - end Mar '24]

§ 31. INSURANCE DE-MYSTIFIED

One should have innate belief in the concept of insurance

As it combines probabilities of many to cover
individuals' risk expanse

But complicated claim calculations and incentivising
claim reduction is the problem

For higher profits, hapless claimants get detrimentally
affected by this dictum

Sadly dis-illusioned, are the existing/potential policy holders
at this delusional bromance

[Context: Insurance Necessity and Claims, re: my own claim - end Mar '24]

§ 32. HEALTHY CONTRARIAN VIEWS

For their actions, humans are forever seeking logical acceptance

For their wrong moves, they hope to avoid their comeuppance

Rewards and punishments are natural as
man(woman) is a social animal

Always seeking company that is pleasant and desirable

But not one's clone - wants healthy discussion
with different view and stance

*[Context: Humans' needs for rewards(punishments), and
healthy debates - end Mar '24]*

§ 33. OFFENSE TO COUNTER DEFENCE

It is often said that Offence is the best strategy of Defence

Politicians do so by diverting issues, whataboutery and keeping atmosphere tense

Reducing unemployment is possibly the foremost issue to be discussed

But they are busy trading jibes at one another and being cussed

Voters have to be alert and not get swayed either way, seeing issues through a sharp lens

[Context: No meaningful TV or Election Campaign Debates - early Apr '24]

§ 34. 'AAYAA RAAM, GAYAA RAAM'

Why are opposition members leaving and going over to the ruling regime?

Is it moral turpitude or no scruples left, nor compunction of loss of ideology or esteem?

Or is it loss of ticket, lure of money and/or position, or fear of the agencies?

'Cos almost everyone has some skeletons, especially public office s/he who fancies

If saddened by current party, fight independently, to follow and be honest to own dream

[Context: Ideology bereft, hopping politicians - early Apr '24]

§ 35. 'CLEAN' ELECTIONS

Let's pray that the 'atmosphere' for the national
elections remains 'clean'

'Clean Atmosphere' both, as in the weather and in
the campaigning/results scene

Am echoing/supporting Ms Dia Mirza's hope that
our 'environment' shouldn't get 'vitiated'

The process should remain healthy, vibrant, fair - and
not get hijacked or deviated

Pinning hope that all - political parties, candidates,
voters, agencies, remain vigilant & keen

[Context: 'Clean Atmosphere' needed - early Apr '24]

§ 36. ELECTIONMANIA

Elections, elections, elections - just lies, boasts and promises

Whether opposition or ruling regime, all are
same - there are no surprises

Real issues like unemployment are not being cracked

By raising trivial issues, these are being side-tracked

Electorate to be blamed too - almost everyone
acquiesces but compromises

[Context: Electorate needs to be alert and is ultimately responsible for sifting out the chaff from the grain - mid Apr '24]

§ 37. JUSTICE DELAYED - INJUSTICE OR JUSTICE DENIED?

Has anyone thought, how it is to be acquitted after 27 jail years?

Pride may be restored a bit but life is shattered and in 'tears'

If evidence was insufficient, then, earlier, both
the investigators and courts had erred

Penalise both as a deterrent, since the accused
had indelibly and unfairly suffered

Softening impact: To start life anew, pay sufficient
compensation, which the State bears

[Context: A person acquitted after 27 years in prison - mid Apr '24]

§ 38. DIVERSE VOICES NEEDED!!

With independent-minded JNU and Jamia Millia academic institutions

There was always hope about vibrant dialogues,
debates and healthy fusions

Funded by the Centre's UCC, it seemed that Govt. was
interested in counter viewpoints

But inundating rigid minded people in one and
choking funds of such coaching joints

A question arises on the Govt's genuine open-mindedness and
its true intentions

[Context: Jamia Millia's Coaching Institute's funds choked - mid Apr '24]

§ 39. EVM-VVPAT SPAT

With the EVM (Electronic Voting Machine) and
VVPAT (Voter Verified Paper Audit Trail) debate ensuing

With all EVMs having VVPAT, norm should be random
X% check via VVPAT, for every constituency voting

Plus, if difference by EVM between winner and next is
very close, say Y%(or 1%), VVPAT check must be done

'Displaying' further fairness, paper trail should be
visible to the voter after voting, even if not given

Besides these, if any very exceptional/unusual issue
crops up, EC should resort to VVPAT re-counting

[Context: Possible solution to the perennial EVM- VVPAT debate - mid Apr '24]

§ 40. PROPORTIONAL REPRESENTATION DEMOCRACY

Proportional representation democracy should
be based on vote share/percentage

National party with highest vote share should
get EC's invite to come centre stage

But not less than 30% should be the vote share of
the national party under consideration

For EC to give to this party, between 52 and 55%
of the Lok Sabha seats' distribution

Proportional representation to others, giving simple majority with
robust opposition, for healthy democratic visage

*[Context: Introspection for a better democratic system, due to
misuse/abuse of provisions*

§ 41. CAMPAIGNING QUALITY, A NEW LOW!

Unfortunately, murky campaigning has become par for
the course, these days, in an election

Sadly, there's fast progress in mouthing blatant lies,
imputed motives, family slander and personal vilification

All are equal culprits; no single party is absolved from such wrong doing

Be it cadres, leaders or incumbent office holders - true
colours of all are showing

The EC of T Seshan's autonomous legacy has lost its bite, and
is now only a mute dispensation

[Context: Nadir in electioneering quality, with a pliant/mute EC - early May '24]

§ 42. CHANGED NOTATION OF 'NOTA'

Nota Bene (N.B.) in Latin, at the suffix means 'Please Note'

NOTA, however, means, 'None Of The Above', deserves my vote

Earlier, if NOTA received the highest vote, the election
had to be reconstituted

Changed rule, however, declares the second highest
candidate, as elected

Marauding the intentions, making the change, a
sarcastic GOAT (Greatest Of All Time)

[Context: Change brought about by EC in NOTA's 'concept' - early May '24]

§ 43. CURRENT EC'S 'SPINE'

Like T Seshan, current CEC and EC needs to 'take the bull by the horns' and step out of its comfort zone

Be it to tackle party hopping destroyers, liars, defaulters or campaign rousers - spiny skills, it needs to hone

With strict SOPs and equal execution, both ruling regime and opposition need to be made compliant

The 'dirt' in politics, getting murkier, it needs to show its fangs and not look the other way and be pliant

For Democracy, Nation and its People, if this moment is passed by, by the EC, it will have only itself to blame and moan

[Context: EC's lip-service and uneven notices to BJP and INC - end May '24]

§ 44. THE GREAT EQUALIZER – INDIAN ELECTIONS 2024

Politically, Indian Elections 2024 have brought about a great equalization

Electorate has decidedly and rightfully ushered in a strong opposition

Landslide and runaway victories usually bring about a cult phenomena

Such persona tends to become an egotistic, power intoxicated prima donna

For progress with checks, along with strong opposition, ideal is simple majority, maybe a small coalition

[Context: Balanced actual result (instead of Landslide Exit Poll) of Indian Elections 2024 - early Jun '24]

THEME 3

INTERNATIONAL ARENA

§ 1. CONFLICT POCKETS

Hamas-Israel, like Ukraine-Russia conflicts are needlessly stretching on
Whole cities and families are totally devastated and forlorn
Aggression with more aggression does not prove anyone right
Only leaves vox populi with a dreadful and ghastly sight
Leaving societal fabric diseased, impoverished, asunder and torn

[Context: International conflicts (Israel-Hamas/Palestine, Russia-Ukraine stretching on and on - early Nov '23]

§ 2. HOS (HEADS OF STATES)

Most HOS (Heads of State) are pretentious Who's Who -
one of their own kinds of an adversary

'Tis a tale of three of them, of dubious, fallacious persona -
a Mr Z (Zee), Mr P and a Mr B

While old B has a global writ, debt makes him hollow inside

P has a tough facade with a valid point about
doorstep enemy on the side

Finally, young macho, stubborn and dependant for war i.e. your Mr Z

[Context: Russia-Ukraine war and US (Zelenskyy, Putin, Biden) - end Nov '23]

§ 3. MID-EAST FLARE-UP

H and I are next to each other but do not see eye to eye
H precedes I and tunnelled through but I's retaliation has gone very high
Jews, in the past, had been wronged massively
But 2 States Theory can't be wished away viciously
Palestinians, select wisely, otherwise your dreams may needlessly die

[Context: Israel leader going overboard (possibly for elections) in Israel-Hamas/ Palestine war - mid Dec '23]

§ 4. USA'S PREDICAMENT

Foremost country's Heads, one after another are being subjected to impeachment
Is it lack of ethics and morals or designed mis-management?
Both hail from parties of different hues and ideologies
For a leading country, it is a matter of shame, not of eulogies
A rather nadir state of affairs, such dubious attainment

[Context: Both party's Leaders state of affairs in USA - mid Dec '23]

§ 5. MALDIVIAN SAGA

'Clownish' comments/posts for any Head of State are
downright rude and obnoxious

Coming from ministers of another country, these are
highly deplorable and outrageous

More so, emanating from a country that has been
helped and is a small neighbour

Size, however, is not the issue - question is of self-respect,
decorum, prestige and honour

No reply, no attack but shunning the oft-visited, by all,
is a befitting response and courageous

[Context: Maldives' minister's dastardly comments on India's PM - mid Jan '24]

§ 6. USA CONSTITUTION

With changing times, it seems the US of A constitution needs a tweak

Unfolding events in recent years showcase the
need for law makers to speak

Three months prior and post the elections, the
Presidency should become a 'Caretaker' one

Devoid of the all-comprehensive presidential immunity,
scrutiny will be fairer on every action

Power of undue influence and whipping up passions
will be subdued and weak

*[Context: ex-USA President, Trump, trying to use Presidential immunity
logic in his legal case - early Feb '24]*

§ 7. 'BIBI'HAWK PRETENSE

Israel, under Bibi, seems to be reneging on the
agreed 'two state' theory

But for personal survival/stature of Israeli hawks,
Gaza was to be given full Palestinian autonomy

By constructing new settlements and apparent
control, Israel's reluctance only built trust deficit

Giving excuse to radicals to become active, reactive,
vengeful and deeply complicit

Such control by Israel makes both peoples suffer
daily and the situation needlessly thorny

[Context: Netanyahu(Bibi) not accepting the agreed 2-nation theory on Palestine - end Feb '24]

§ 8. USA 2024!

Repeats are not always lacklustre, dull, or
disappointing but this one surely is

Election candidates in largest economy - one is
oldest, other diabolical - no excitement, no fizz

One: should have groomed a successor as question marks
are on his alertness and sharpness

Two: an alternative should have emerged to counter
his sexism, chauvinism, rudeness, craftiness

Poor electorate, choice is between the devil and
deep blue sea, between a puzzle and a quiz

[Context: 2024 USA Presidential election likely to repeat the same candidates from both sides - early Mar '24]

§ 9. MID-EAST MAYHEM

The mid-east conflict is getting from bad to worse

From two (Israel, Palestinians/Hamas), it has become a threesome (Iran) curse

Isolated for escalation, even internally, Israel's being held responsible

But think, minus arrogance and ego, would this have been probable

Hospitals nurse, cars/ships traverse - but alas! all are turning into a large hearse

[Context: In the Israel-Hamas war, Israel bombarding hospitals, and Iran entering the fray - mid Apr '24]

§ 10. PALESTINE STATEHOOD RE-QUERIED

UNGA's backing for full membership to Palestine State echoes the accepted 2-state theory

Which the current Israeli dispensation is negating and needlessly turning it gory

In principle, earlier accepted at Camp David but hawkish election focus is on display

Surprisingly, USA voted against the resolution, possibly own monied Jewish lobby at play

India was for the motion, being foremost in recognising Palestine, years ago - will it be or not? Out is the jury

[Context: UN's quandary on Palestine Nation - mid May '24]

§ 11. INDIAN EPIC RE-PLAYED

Today while watching Shrimad Ramayan episode on the meeting between Raam and Vibheeshan

I recollected two past parallels between India & Bangladesh and India & PLO, Palestine Liberation Organization

India's then PM, Indira Gandhi helped liberate Bangladeshis from Pak soldiers' tyranny, and supported Mujibur Rahman as their new leader

Like Raam's empathy for Lankans and crowning Vibheeshan in exile; Yasser Arafat of PLO too was supported when Palestinians had no land to gather

Siding with the right, liberation sans annexation, showed India's and its leader's true ethical intention

[Context: Episode of Vibhheshan meeting Raam in Shri Ramayan serial - and its similarities - end May '24]

§ 12. CONTROVERSIES GET REPEATED

'Rasputin', a controversial figure died in 1916 but still lives in people's mind

Allegations were of religious heresy, closeness to Czar and Czarina, and his political bind

Undue influence on Nicolas II; Aristocrats and Church opposed this Siberian peasant

Plot to kill this mystic 'Mad Monk' fast tracked the Russian Revolution nascent

Autocratic control, opposers' decimation, simmering revolution has parallels of another kind

[Context: Controversial figures and their repetitiveness - end May '24]

§ 13. 'TRUMP'ED BY THE JURY

'Jury is out' means conclusion uncertain but in the US,
the jury clearly 'Trump'ed its verdict

On not 1 but 34 counts, the Manhattan jury found him to be a convict

Though speedy and impartial trial has given
credibility to US justice system

Surprisingly, US presidential system is silent, allows
convicts to contest for role at the helm

So, the quandary is, are the systems not well thought out,
nonpartisan, lenient or strict?

[Context: Jury's Conviction of Ex-USA President, Donald Trump - early Jun '24]

THEME 4

(A)POLITICALLY CORRECT

§ 1. ELECTORAL BONDS' ENIGMA

Opacity, Translucency or Transparency
Is the current Electoral Bonds' enigmatic story
Even unwittingly, recipients get bound by the Bonds' bonding
Later hounding spectre of quid pro quo comes out unfolding
Million dollar/crores rupees question Supreme Court poses -
To be or not to be?!

[Context: SC's initial comments on Electoral Bonds - early Nov '23]

§ 2. CHANAKYA LIKE

Irrespective of ideologies, it would be incorrect not to applaud
And give the two at the helm, even if a reluctant salutation nod
For the strategy of planning and timing
everything for maximising benefit
A la Chanakyasque mindset, to retain power, while
partymen follow the writ
Whipping national fervour, using all which is in control,
so no one can roughshod

[Context: Political Chanakya Strategies being rolled out by ruling regime - mid Dec '23]

§ 3. RELIGIO-POLITICO MIX

Religion-Politics mix is a very dangerous concoction

Grandstanding one religion over others can
lead to uncalled consternation

Great statesmen do not let personal faith and
religion make them myopic

Good national governance should be spiritual and religion-agnostic

Destination is one, paths many, Creator too gave that option

[Context: Ayodhya Temple Inauguration - mid Jan '24]

§ 4. LEVERAGING RELIGION

Past issues aside, new Ayodhya Mandir, for all
Hindus, symbolizes pride and respect

But spending huge taxpayer funds and the fanfare
makes one circumspect

Religion is personal, not showy, especially for the
HoS - causes needless frenzy

Is also fraught with partisanship, divisiveness, and
repercussions crazy

Seers, pundits and acharyas, should be in the forefront,
in all religious aspect

[Context: Ayodhya Temple Inauguration - mid Jan '24]

§ 5. POWER NARCISSISM

'Power corrupts, Absolute power corrupts absolutely '
Fans an egotist, makes him a narcissist eventually
'Tis a saying borne out by human nature examples
In the past and contemporary, there are real life samples
In democracy, fault lies with electorate, in
kingship ruler rules ruthlessly

[Context: Egotist Statements by Top Leader - mid Jan '24]

§ 6. MUM & MAYHEM

Yes, it is wrong when needless disruptions in Parliament
are not discouraged
But by orchestrated release and garlanding of
gang rapists, ponder, who all are encouraged?
Whilst using expletives in public life should be strictly out of bounds
Equally sad, mum's the word, if own party does so or
atrocity in a state abounds
It is not a good reading for any side, now or later when
history papers are rummaged

[Context: Top Leader's silence on certain issues - end Jan '24]

§ 7. USURPED!

'Mahatma' Gandhi Usurped, tho' ideologically shot at, partition derided

'Sardar' Patel Usurped, tho' he unified states, now
divided as UTs/trifurcated

'Netaji' Subhash Bose Usurped, tho' INA (Indian National Army)
is now Agniveer 'contractual' force

'Babasaheb' Ambedkar Usurped, tho' his Buddhist Constitutional
spirit is now way out of course

Playing religious/regional card, mouthing impoliteness, even has
own 'Atal's' eloquent decorum gutted

*[Context: Triggered on Mahatma Gandhi's Death Anniversary,
30th Jan - end Jan '24]*

§ 8. PARLIAMENTARY VIS-À-VIS PRESIDENTIAL FORM

Few years ago, the present ruling party had mooted a change:
Parliamentary to Presidential government

Any party piggy-backing on the aura of one person is
bound to favour such an arrangement

Pros and cons are there in any type of democratic governance

Opposition parties bereft of any towering/unifying
person cannot take such a chance

Complex equations, Opposition frayed; Proportional
Representation seems a better constitutional firmament

*[Context: Ongoing debate on the type of democracy and ruling
regime's tendencies - end Jan '24]*

§ 9. BHARAT RATNA

Like toffees and candies, in 2024, Bharat Ratnas are being doled out

Even to those ideologically opposed, just for
impacting national election bout

Since this was not done in past ten years but
now, it is not magnanimity

It is apparent to all, this is Machiavellian manipulation,
not strategic 'shrewdity'

Depicting a crafty mind, inherent fear and weakness; and
not the confidence of the stout

[Context: Announcement and conferring of many Bharat Ratnas at one go for political mileage - mid Feb '24]

§ 10. (E)G(O)RANTEE

A leader will be humbly respected when s/he says,
"WE will aspire to make/do the best"

Not when s/he claims that it is "MY guarantee" or
"in MY tenure, we reached the crest"

Greatness comes not from self-centred egoism and jingoism

Nor from "I am the best, whom no one can surpass" egotism

If so, love and success will be short-lived, and
history will put her/him to rest

[Context: I Vs the We Guarantees - mid Feb '24]

§ 11. RELIGIOUS MONUMENTS

Professed non-Hindu and theocratic countries are permitting building of Hindu temple with its spire

Whilst in professed secular ones, ironically, churches and mosques are increasingly coming under fire

Circumstances, tho' are different, the first is driven by an outward outlook, and Indian diaspora's contribution

The other is driven by history - alleged razing of temples, building mosques, and now their restoration

Religiosity, a faith of mind, is in helping the needy, alas, not in wasting money on building grandiose structure

[Context: Saudi Arabia & UAE allows building of Hindu temples Vs litigation on religious structures in India - mid Feb '24]

§ 12. PANDERING TO EQ (EMOTIONAL QUOTIENT)

Jai Jawan Jai Kisan was the slogan then, hailing the saviours of our borders and of hunger

Now, Jai Bhagwan has gained pre-election prominence, pandering to the EQ number

Religiosity and Spiritualism is not bad per se but mix with politics is

Wearing Religion on the sleeve with photo ops as the new election mantra, has become rizz

Thereby, playing with people's emotions and making rationality, values, logic go asunder

[Context: Photo Ops and Elections importance to One Religion - early Mar '24]

§ 13. PRE-ELECTION RAZZMATAZZ

Blitzkrieg tours, spate of announcements, barrage of premature inaugurations

Whilst people wait eagerly for the dates of the national, Lok Sabha elections

EC's proclamation of dates will make 'Code of Ethics' the king

Prior doling out of largesse makes circumvention an arty master of the ring

As the 'non-partisan' one-man EC, hurriedly made to three, awaits mutedly for instructions

[Context: Pre-election hurried tours, projects' announcements, inaugurations - mid Mar '24]

§ 14. RULING HIGH-HANDEDNESS

Latent assertiveness on institutions, by ruling regimes, is found everywhere

But blatant high-handedness is borne out of sheer arrogance, and is extremely unfair

In autocracies or similar, though not desirable, such is understandable

But in democracies, such behaviour is unpalatable and unacceptable

Displays a dictatorial streak, fear of backlash and possibly an empty dare

[Context: Sudden spate of political cases, raids and arrests on opposition leaders - end Mar '24]

§ 15. QUID PRO QUO

Slowly but surely as quid pro quo events are
opening up and panning out

It seems Electoral Bonds' Scheme was designed
as a pressure tactic tout

More so when even the highest court has pronounced
it illegal and non-legit

100% onus is on the framers of the scheme to prove
their innocence and show its merit

Sequentiality is enough for a suo moto SC supervised
quick investigation bout

[Context: SC's verdict on Electoral Bonds' invalidity - end Mar '24]

§ 16. INFLEXION POINT, MAYBE

Actions against the opposition, especially the timing,
seems to be that crucial inflexion point

Just before the elections, giving fillip to opposition
unity and keeping them buoyant

Who knows, this miscalculation may ultimately
turn out to be good for the country

Wherein people ponder and vote, for simple majority
of a party, and not giving a runaway victory

To usher in proper governance, having checks and balances,
which is both inclusive and joint

[Context: Agencies' raids on opposition parties/leaders - end Mar '24]

§ 17. PM CARES (Citizen Assistance and Relief in Emergency Situations) FUND

PM Cares Fund, in many ways, is similar to Electoral Bonds' Scheme

Being a Public Charitable Trust, 'tis neither under Parliamentary
scrutiny nor under PIL radar's beam

Framed during Covid pandemic, People/Corporates/PSUs,
in large numbers, were asked to donate

With no details for public scrutiny, 'tis a time bomb
ticking, ready to detonate

And has the footprints of a Machiavellian mind,
with the same non-transparent theme

[Context: Non-transparency of PM CARES Fund instead of PM Relief Fund - early Apr '24]

§ 18. INTERNATIONAL AGREEMENT COMMITMENTS

In world diplomacy, prevailing circumstances drive
the concept of give and take

Raking up international agreements, years later,
reeks of desperation and is a big mistake

Just to divert attention, counter own silence and
gain brownie points with the electorate

Wanting to dishonour nation's commitments,
and decisions of past leaders of the state

Backlash is a strong possibility, with huge
repercussions and arrogant credibility at stake

[Context: Katchatheevu Island Saga, Sri Lanka - early Apr '24]

§ 19. CLANDESTINE OPS

Firstly, clandestine killings of individuals by one country
in another should be a No Go

Even if a one-off is needed for nation's security, it's got
to be in a meticulous, traceless flow

In friendly or enemy country, skilful planning is key,
as a slip can damage nation's credibility

And repeatedly singling out anti-nationals,
points fingers and raises questionability

Loss of sovereign respect can fan 'rogue' nation
theory and conspiracy backlash grow

[Context: Neutralisation in other countries of Nijjar, other anti-Indian terrorists; attempt on Pannun - and Defence Minister (and now PM)'s hinting statements - early Apr '24]

§ 20. ENCOUNTERS

The issue is not about criminals' death - most people
would probably sigh and feel relieved

Encounters, in today's society are a blotch - kangaroo
court like justice is hard to be believed

Crime has no religion - punishment should not be
'street justice' but lawful, after trial

Dastardly crimes should be fast tracked - then the
verdict may be the noose or poison vial

Civil society should not resort to extra judicial methods,
later rule of law will be hard to be retrieved

[Context: 'Encounters' on criminals in the country - early Apr '24]

§ 21. I/ME/MYSELF SYNDROME

Elections, especially, should portray and
display Humility, the true Hinduism trait

Not arrogance and ego and boastfulness of 'Me/I am
the greatest of the great'

Unfortunately, increasingly, the collective noun of
'We/Our' is losing its primacy

When all of the past is derided, and there is a sense
of 'Only, I can deliver' obduracy

Remember, elections are not about 'one person'
but the stature of our Great Indian State

[Context: 'I/Me' taking over all discourse - early Apr '24]

§ 22. IMPARTIAL VOICES REQUIRED

It is said that to be honest is not enough, one has to actually show it

Independence, autonomy, impartiality - Judiciary,
EC have to show and do their bit

When Atal ji was PM, EC had his pictures on NHAI
billboards covered during elections

Suo moto or on various objections, there is now
either no or delayed actions

With immediate notice by EC on ruling regime's
petitions, credibility has taken a hit

*[Context: Non-partisanship - EC's differential speeds in different
cases - mid Apr '24]*

§ 23. PEOPLE'S HIGH PERCEPTION TAKES A HIT

With changed circumstances, the PM has indeed
righted many a wrong

With his team, not alone, and with decisiveness, sure and strong

But when show off legacy, arrogance and ego take over

Inappropriate discourse, brings august office's stature, lower

People's perception going down will not take long

[Context: Low quality language decreases people's respect - end Apr '24]

§ 24. UNBRIDLED POWER - ONE EXTREME CAUSE OF POLITICAL ILLS

Unbridled power is the root cause of political ills,
leading to arrogance, fanning egoism

Egoism feeds and nurtures egotism, 'I am always right',
and onwards to narcissism

'Tis true, certain issues require covertness,
matured secrecy; where bragging does no good

The 'could' scenario in Doubting Thomases'
minds becomes a 'should' or a 'would'

For the sake of sycophancy and adulation,
a shroud envelops pragmatism

[Context: PM saying during election campaigning that 'No dossier but will go inside and hit' - early May '24]

§ 25. CONTRIVED INTERVIEWS

There was a time when a top actor had shunned the media,
which had repaid him likewise

Sadly today, media goes gaga on a top leader's scripted interview,
who had no direct interaction otherwise

Brushed under the carpet, virtually no tough counter
questions were asked or possibly allowed

How the interview had been tailored, for some common
people too, it came out clear and loud

Not 4th estate, hard hitting journalism but TRPs, Campaign
compulsions seem to have led to this awkward compromise

[Context: Leader, who did not have a single press conference in 10 years, agrees to give 'interviews' to select media during election time - end May '24]

§ 26. HYPOTHETICAL BRAGGING

When it's said that Kartarpur should've been taken
back in 1971, it's just playing to the gallery

People should see through the false electoral bravado
and not put the speaker in a pillory

Then, economy wasn't healthy, military equipment quite basic,
both east-west borders needed defending

The other side had support of the US, eastern people were being
liberated sans annexation, and 7th Fleet approaching

When conditions were adverse and different, why this needless
comparison and words' battery?

Context: PM's remarks at election rally in Punjab on hypothesis of taking back Kartarpur, during 1971 war - end May '24]

THEME 5

FESTIVELY FATHOMED

§ 1. VISHWAKARMA DAY

On this auspicious day of Shri Vishwakarma
May all lives be filled with good karma
Workers even down their tools in obeisance
With vows of no cheating, no malfeasance
Praying for rulers and leaders to be rooted in the terra firma

[Context: Concept of Vishwakarma Day - mid Sep '23]

§ 2. 'KARWA CHAUTH'

It is quite a unique festival in India called 'Karwa Chauth'
Prior to difficult moon rise, wives do not
partake even water or broth
They fast for their husbands' welfare
But likewise, husbands do not do their share
Such inequity makes the old man, Rabbali, fume and froth

[Context: 'Karwa Chauth' one-sided fasting - end Oct '23]

§ 3. HARVESTING START

Lohri/Makar Sankranti/Pongal/Khichdi/Uttarayanan/Maghi/Magh
Bihu - many names, one occasion

Beauty of India - diversified celebrations in one nation

Invoking Fire and Sun gods, praying for good
harvest is the common belief

Lohri, in cold north is dancing, singing, revdi (candy),
peanuts, popcorn amidst bonfire relief

Not only India, other countries too, like Bulgaria,
have similar harvesting tradition

[Context: Concept behind 'Lohri' - mid Jan '24]

§ 4. HARDWAR IS HARI-DWAR

The religious city, Haridwar, means 'Gateway to God'

'Har ki paudi' is actually 'Hari ki paudi' i.e. 'Steps to the Lord'

Performing the final rites in the 'Ganga', people
get emotionally drenched

'Tis said that here hunger and thirst of ancestors
is spiritually quenched

Here juxtaposition of beautiful 'aarti', piousness,
beggary, pollution seems quite odd

[Context: The piousness, relevance and 'scene' at Haridwar - early Feb '24]

§ 5. AUSPICIOUS TRINE

What an overlap this year! - 3 major religions combine
to form an auspicious trine

Lent started mid Feb, will culminate with Good Friday on Mar 29

Mar 8 was Maha Shivratri & Women's Day, followed
by start of Ramadan Kareem

On 25 Mar, ongoing Lent and Ramzan, will witness Holi,
the festival of colours, in between

Rozas end with Eid ul Fitr, Navratras start for Raam Navmi
by mid Apr - 'tis divine and sublime

[Context: 3 major religions' main festivals falling in the same period in early 2024 - mid Mar '24]

§ 6. HOLY HOLI

Holi, the festival of colours, is indeed very holy

And is also full of Krishn mischief and madness, a la folie

Belief craziness: Atheist king Hiranyakashyap Vs
Prahlad, his Believer son

Who was asked to sit in fire by his father but he
remained unburnt and won

And saved the day with his innate trust of The Lord,
like a good life goalie

[Context: Significance of Holika Dahan and Holi - end Mar '24]

§ 7. EASTER WEEKEND!

As per history, Jesus Christ was crucified on Friday,
called Good Friday!

'Good' 'cos He was ready to sacrifice Himself for
entire humanity, come what may

The burden of cross He carried was actually the
burden of evil, of mankind

They nailed Him to the cross and let Him die but could
not kill His thoughts and purity of mind

Heavens cried, Lepers recovered, His Resurrection
happened for our benefit, on Easter Sunday!

[Context: Why Christ's Death is 'Good' in the Easter period - end Mar '24]

§ 8. 1st APRIL - FOOL's DAY

Though the genesis of Fool's Day on 1st April, is uncertain

Be careful, just a jest is fine, but it should not hurt,
drawing up a curtain

Emergency services, like Fire, Police getting
frivolous and dubious calls;

Waste critical resources, and are in bad taste, definitely not LOLs

Light-hearted pranks, in right spirit can cultivate
bonhomie sweet and certain

[Context: Origins of Fool's Day on 1st of April - early Apr '24]

§ 9. SIGNIFICANCE OF CHAITRA NAVRATRI & RAAM NAVMI

Chaitra Navratri ushers in spring, along with Maa Durga and her nine incarnations' celebration

In different eras, Lord Vishnu took human form as Lord Raam (on Raam Navmi, 9th day) and earlier as Matsya(fish) reincarnation

This Chaitra, the Hindu New Year, Samvat 2081 (57 years ahead of the Gregorian) starts, with festive appeal & happiness

Also, herein, Lord Brahma created the Universe, and with Sun at its highest, there is unity, joy and zestful peppiness

This showcases Hinduism's social values, cultural heritage, and peaceful orientation

[Context: Mar/Apr's (Chaitra) Navratri and Raam Navmi's beliefs enumerated - early Apr '24]

§ 10. IMPORTANCE OF RAMZAN & EID-UL-FITR

Eid-ul-Fitr is the festive end of the 9th/fasting month of Islamic calendar, Ramzan or Ramadan

Prophet Mohammed received enlightenment from the Heavens, captured in the Holy book, Quran

It is the book of guidance for both men and women, giving directives for salvation

Which is similar to the other Holy books of other religions that also lead to such revelation

All religions are different paths to same destination, exhorted by Gurus and muezzin's call, Azaan

[Context: Ramadan and Eid-ul-Fitr's significance - early Apr '24]

§ 11. DR. AMBEDKAR JAYANTI

Salutations to Dr. Babasaheb Ambedkar on his
birth anniversary (14th April)!

Like the new harvest of Baisakhi, and the new solar year,
he was a new luminary

Hindu turned Buddhist, representing the Dalits,
secular, erudite, outspoken, intelligent

Indian Constitution was made under his able
leadership of the Assembly Constituent

Constitution Book, a document finesse, was nurtured by him
very thoughtfully and definitely not cursory

[Context: 'Father' of Indian Constitution, Dr Babasaheb Ambedkar's relevance on his birthversary - 140424]

§ 12. 'SURYA TILAK'

Yesterday's 'Surya tilak' at the new Ram Temple at
Ayodhya was indeed a sight to behold

Similar to sun rays at the southern tip, entering
at old Kanya Kumari's edifice's fold

Whether the timing, on the last day of the 1st
phase campaigning was intentional or otherwise

I am of strong belief, as shown numerously, across
the world - mixing religion with politics is not wise

It has the propensity to cause dogmatism, mayhem, conflicts untold

[Context: Sun's rays anointing the new Ram Temple in Ayodhya, and mixing religion & politics - mid Apr '24]

§ 13. BHAGWAN MAHAVIR'S PHILOSOPHY

On Mahavir Jayanti, salutations to the followers of Jainism

The 24th Teerthankar, a great seer, who at age 30,
went into asceticism

Bhagwan Mahavir, also known as Vardhman was against
the Attribution Syndrome

I.e. passing the buck of our actions to the
'Power' created by us, in Heaven

He said that only we are responsible for our actions,
and that is the absolute truism

[Context: Highlighting 24th Guru of Jains, Bhagwan Mahavir's 'Attribution Syndrome' philosophy on his birthversary - end Apr '24]

§ 14. JAI HANUMAAN!

Best wishes to everyone on Shri Hanumaan's birthday,
Hanumaan Jayanti

Belief has it, with infinitesimal soul of Lord Shiva,
he was son of god of wind, and called Maruti

Not only was He one of the mightiest
combinations of brains and brawn

But was also an eternal servitor of Lord Vishnu
'avataar', Bhagwan Raam

And possibly the inspiration behind Super Heroes
of today, to save humanity

[Context: Super Hero Hanumaan ji re-visited on his birthversary - end Apr '24]

§ 15. MAY DAY - DOUBLE IMPACT

May Day, a flummoxing term - is it World Labour Day or
an SOS (Save our Soul) call?

Haymarket Riot on 4th May 1886 in Chicago, remembered
as Labour Day from 1st May 1889, thru Trade Unions' gall

'Desperate saving call' by mariners or pilots is heralded
by "Mayday, Mayday, Mayday"

To goad into swift action, those who are at play,
oblivious to dangers at bay

In essence, both are 'saving' calls - for human rights,
and for human lives, trying to avoid a bigger 'squall'

[Context: Labour Day & May Day significance - 010524]

§ 16. 'AKSHAYA TRITYA' MULTI-SIGNIFICANCE

Akshaya, the imperishable, also Raavan's younger son;
and Tritya, the third moon phase, in Baisakh

Many legends make this day - birth of Maa Annapurna;
killing of demon Mahishasur by Maa Durga's sword arc

And birth of Parshuram-6th 'avataar' of Lord Vishnu;
also unveiling of 'Ganga'/Ganges, India's water lifeline

Ganesh ji's recitation of Mahabharat epic to Ved Vyas;
and start of Tretaa Yug divine

Poor Sudama's humble visit to childhood friend Krishn; Krishn's
'akshay paatr'/pot of unending food for Pandavs' exiled days dark

*[Context: People's celebration of this day every year, without
truly knowing the reason/s - mid May '24]*

§ 17. EONS/'YUGS' SIMPLY PUT

Each cycle of 4,320,000 years consists of 4 eons or yugs - Krita or
Satya, Tretaa, Dwaapar, and Kaali

First was Satya Yug, with prevalence of Truth in thoughts, words
and deeds, partaking 'saatvik'/pure food, daily

Love and Righteousness was the crux of Tretaa Yug, as epitomised
by Raam, Lord Vishnu's reincarnation

Krishn, another Lord Vishnu-The Preserver's reincarnation,
in Dwaapar Yug, espoused 'Karma', doing deeds
without result expectation

Current, Kaali Yug, in the face of corruption
and pollution, exhorts us unsuccessfully, to follow
Prakash/Light of being egoless, very humbly

[Context: Kaali Yug negativities - mid May '24]

THEME 6

FRAGMENTAL FOCUS

§ 1. MAHUA SAGA

Whilst there is the small, showy Mexican Chihuahua
Indians have their own medicinal alcoholic plant Mahua
The Mexican is sought-after, beautiful, energetic but a bark sans bite
The Indian bark is remedial, with opposers rattled,
piqued and ready to fight
Our feisty, gutsy, Mahua scores miles over the others, Voila!

[Context: Mahua Moitra saga in Parliament - end Oct '23]

§ 2. LIQUORGATE SCANDAL

Liquorgate has seen many heads roll in the duty of Excise
From the bottom to top it is a tornado-spiralling exercise
Opposition claims it is a clinic-less mohalla
And schools too are a clue-less halla
In the docks, the 'affected' are perplexed about ways to exorcise

[Context: BJP and AAP counter-charges on Delhi's healthcare clinics and Govt. schools - end Oct '23]

§ 3. POLL OUTCOME

Finally, after some wait, the poll results are out
Blame game will start by losers, to create a doubt
The results are quite different from the psephologists' reckoning
Iffy states had decisive mandates and unexpected landslide acoming
Introspection or not, Pundits & Parties will get ready for the next bout

[Context: 5 States Vidhan Sabha/Assembly polls - early Dec '23]

§ 4. WALK-A-THON

The 'Justice Tour' is exactly that: 'Just Ice To Our' 'young turk' walker

Kudos for trying to break the ice, tho' white
Tees are the focussed stalker

Who is attempting to re-connect to the roots, and
build a groundswell of goodwill

Kudos, from their perspective, opponents focus
on inanities, going for the kill

Main issues are getting derailed,
sadly losing the way, is this Marathoner?

[Context: Rahul Gandhi's Nyay Yatra from east to west - mid Jan '24]

§ 5. INCORRECT FOCUS

Long-term survival of a group needs a minimum agenda
benefitting the common person

Removal of one man should not be the singularly focussed reason

'Cos when a person goes, another of his ilk, more
dogmatic could get the role

But if the common man identifies with the agenda,
no other can take the position pole

This is the pure and true dynamics of creating a conducive plan of action

[Context: INDIA Bloc's initial one-point, Modi removal agenda - mid Jan '24]

§ 6. INDIA BLOC

The opposition INDIA Bloc is getting increasingly blocked

Procrastination seems the reason for getting internally rocked

Recent assembly results were a rude shock

On which there was much dependence of the bloc

The ruling party played smart and has them out-knocked

*[Context: INDIA Bloc losing its way (in the aftermath of the Assembly
elections' results? - end Jan '24]*

§ 7. BIHARI TWISTS & TURNS

Once there was a man from the 'enlightened' state
of Taxila-fame Bihar

Unparalleled deftness he had in making u-turns,
in the quest for power

Like the proverbial cat's lives, he took HoS oath
for a record ninth time

Machiavelli guile, even with minority support,
used to position himself ruler prime

Power equations are usually complex, unprincipled,
not straight and linear

[Context: Nitish Kumar's manouevering and machinations (with UPA, then NDA/BJP, then against/INDIA Bloc, then again NDA/BJP) - early Feb '24]

§ 8. 'SO RAN'

There was a man, 'So Ran' he somewhere that ED could not nab

They looked everywhere for over 6 hrs but could not put a tab

He surfaced in his home town, on his own

Called party members for crucial decision, in his dome

For electing next HoS, surrendered, mocked they could not grab

[Context: Hemant Soren dodging ED before surrendering - early Feb '24]

§ 9. OPPOSITION LOSING STEAM

In the 17th Lok Sabha, even amidst the pandemic,
some good decisive actions occurred

Some indelible forgettables: Farmers' stir, Egotist
propaganda, whilst Manipuris suffered

Most commendable was the unanimous
passing of the Women's Reservation Bill

New Parliament building, hosting G 20 and Ayodhya temple -
the government went for the kill

Opposition gained some momentum in its mission
but sadly remained vision-blurred

[Context: INDIA Bloc opposition's dithering, meandering, slow concerted effort - mid Feb '24]

§ 10. SANDESH-KHALI

Not 'khaali sandesh'(empty message) but 'sandesh kaala' (black
message) is received from Sandeshkhali, Bengal

Gladder will be the 'junta'(populace) if surgical
'operation bladder' is done, to remove mafia's gall

Minority vote bank patronage is the RCA (root cause analysis)
for this 'gunda' fiefdom's existence

Where loot of the body(rape) is carried out with gay abandon,
killing both soul and conscience

Dons' heads will have to roll swiftly, at the altar of majority
vote bank, to put The Mother(nay, Sister) Company again
on a roll, having a ball

[Context: West Bengal's Sandeshkhali mass rape episode - end Feb '24]

§ 11. MISGUIDED MISSILES

It is not that Opposition does not have real
issues to confront, like unemployment

But every other day, one of them remark, like on
PM's Hinduism - a bad taste comment

De-focussing from main pain points, permitting
government to set its narrative

Media capitalizes on such spicy trivia debates,
for garnering TRPs/eyeballs massive

Electorate is the loser, core topics remain
unanswered as discussions go into a tangent

[Context: Needless comment, like on PM's Hinduism, facilitates ruling party to digress from main issues - early Mar '24]

§ 12. HONESTY IS TO BE FELT, NOT SHOUTED

Self-professed 'pure and honest', CM in the docks

No smoke without fire - the smoke teases and mocks

Total privatization of liquor sales, with higher margins

Questions rightly raised by self-proclaimed, 'guardians'

Introspecting, CM reverses policy and still feels he rocks?

[Context: Delhi CM's new liquor policy reversal, and having to shout about his honesty - end Mar '24]

§ 13. PLAYING THE MARTYR

Does a CM think that elections can be won by
playing the victim card or martyr?

Depends on emotional connect - either a total
dud or winning bark of a bull terrier

Sympathy vote or negative perception - depends
on electorate's comprehension

Events, circumstances, track record, 'crying wolf' -
all will guide their voting action

Lack of explanation by CM, wrong timing
by ruling regime - who will be much the merrier?

[Context: Delhi CM's arrest by ED on Liquorgate scandal - end Mar '24]

§ 14. RELIGIOUS CLASHES - A SHAME!

Clashes on any religious festival are a huge
blemish on Indian diversity

Hits at the very roots of the proud Hindu
tolerance and respected secularity

Be it Bengal, Kerala, Gujarat, J&K or MP,
the onus lies with state governments

To ensure proper procedures, monitoring,
security at any of such events

If SOPs are not made and adhered unbiasedly,
it would be tantamount to justice travesty

[Context: Religious clashes in West Bengal - mid Apr '24]

§ 15. DELINEATION OF POWER

President is our Constitutional Head and Prime Minister,
Head of Govt., with domains duly defined

Similar roles for Governors/LGs and Chief Ministers,
in the states, are outlined

These days, needless tussle arises when CM is not from Centre's
party - similar at the Centre is dealt with maturity

Paralysis sets in, everything goes to the SC,
which has to decide the parity

PWD's delays are caused likewise, common
man suffers and finds himself in a bind

[Context: Counter narratives on Garbage landfill, state of roads, delay in completion of infra projects, in Delhi - mid Apr '24]

§ 16. INCORRECT TIMING

The harbinger of India's Telecom Revolution in the 1980/1990s -
what's happened to him?

His recent utterances and 'politically incorrect'
remarks are witted quite dim

Not a member but close association generates
unfavourable narrative for the political party

Especially in these super-charged national election times,
there is needless negative publicity

Whether it is senility or taken out of context,
other side takes political mileage to the brim

[Context: Sam Pitroda's comments on Estate Duty in USA, UK; during India's National/Lok Sabha elections - early May '24]

§ 17. 'RESERVATIONS' - A HELPING HAND TO THE DOWNTRODDEN

Reservation was introduced for the Harijans/oppressed castes -
based on religion, is a step regressive

Islam with no caste system should proudly consider itself progressive

75 years of Independence, irrespective of any religion, gravitation must be
towards poverty linked reservation

And not micro-fragmenting the society into further divisions and
pockets of seclusion

Social justice and equity, and not religious vote bank politics
should be the reason for such a missive

[Context: Lalu's call for religious reservation for muslims - mid May '24]

THEME 7

SPORTINGLY ENTERTAINED

§ 1. ASIA CUP WIN

Team India, Asia cup win, Many Congratulations
Nice mixing, twinning and weathery coagulations
Belief is high for the next world tourney
Over confidence should not mar your onward journey
No flash in the pan this, prove wrong all
naysayers and confabulations

[Context: On India's Asia Cup (Cricket) win - mid Sep '23]

§ 2. WORLD ODI - PREVIOUS WINNER'S FALL

A country which ruled the world but is now just an island
It introduced the game of cricket to the world, i.e. England
It won the ODI cup in 2019, though a controversial decision
Against its erstwhile colony, New Zealand which
is a beautiful nation
In 2023 ODI cup, The UK seems to have become overconfident

[Context: An over-confident UK in World ODI
(One-Day Internationals) - end Oct '23]

§ 3. WORLD ODI - INDIAN SPREE

Indian cricket team in ODI WC is on an unprecedented spree
The ole' man sayeth: Previously it was 1983 and now 2023
Earlier they were minnows, now the richest team
Rich in funds and in talent, many nations aspired dream
Perfect combo for a home run, all envy and agree

[Context: Hoping for World One Day International, ODI mantle for the Indian Team, owing to its fantastic performance -early Nov '23]

§ 4. PROSE IN POETRY

Prose and Song is a difficult combine
But Gulzar and RD are Masters sublime
'Mera kuchh saamaan...' is a beautiful example
Wide-eyed was everyone listening this metered ensemble
What dexterity & finesse, in moulding sentences into a chime!

[Context: Own philosophical Prose and Poetry's amalgam - end Nov '23]

§ 5. BOPANNA'S TENNIS FEAT!

Heartiest Congratulations to our very own
tennis ace, Rohan Bopanna
From a new kid on the block, he becomes a Super 'Anna'(Sir)
At 43, becomes the oldest, World's No. 1 Doubles player
Kudos and tons of platitudes for this mighty slayer
The Singles' Super Anna(Djokovic) also wants
to partner our Prima Donna

[Context: On Bopanna becoming oldest Tennis World's Doubles Player - end Jan '24]

§ 6. GROTESQUE PORTRAYAL

'Animal' received the plaudits and film awards
Humans are animals too but with brains, and not on quads
Though acting was pretty Gothic and commendable,
Grotesque, super-heroic violence was realistically despicable
Inner human-animal display was more graphic, by miles and yards

[Context: 'Animal' Film's grotesque portrayal - early Feb '24]

§ 7. DISTINCTIVE SINGERS

Earlier, there were very distinctive singing voices
Listeners had no issues in distinguishing their choices
Be it Nasal Saigal, Vibrato Talat, Baseful Hemant,
Suave Rafi, Pahadi SD
Or even Yodeling Kishore, Classical MannaDe,
Soulful Mukesh, High pitch Mahendra, Energetic RD
Unlike today, each had a unique timber and tenor, vocal juices

[Context: Erstwhile 'Unique Voiced' Indian singers - early Feb '24]

§ 8. U-19 ODI World Cup

In 2024 edition, U-19 Indian cricketers are scripting history
By their 5th consecutive ODI World Cup finals entry
New talent emerges from such breeding grounds
Some of which goes awry from victory and
some torments and hounds
To keep the proud Indian flag flying high in
cricketing legacy and ancestry

*[Context: Under 19 Indian Cricket Team's 5th consecutive
ODI World Cup entry - early Feb '24]*

§ 9. GRAMMYS

The aura and grammar of the global musical
Grammy Awards is changing greatly

'Best Global Music Album' category has made
Indian musicians and music widespread, proud and stately

Earlier, 'Shakti', 'powered' by Ravi Shankar (sitar), Alla Rakha
(tabla), L Shankar (violin), Vikku (ghatam), were prominent

Now, it's the 'moment' of McLaughlin (guitar), Zakir Hussain
(tabla), Shankar Mahadevan (vocal), Rakesh Chaurasia (flautist),
Rajagopalan (violin) via 'This Moment'

From Carnatic-Hindustani Classical bridging, it is now Jazz-Indian
Classical coming together unabashedly

[Context: On Indian musicians winning Grammy Award - early Feb '24]

§ 10. INDIA'S TRULY FIRST RJ, AMEEN SAYANI

Sadly, another stalwart passed away: the best of RJs,
when that word was not even coined

Doyen of radio, Ameen Sayani's 91 years should
be celebrated, not mourned

Proficient in Hindi-Urdu, an evergreen, fresh silky
voice anchoring Binaca Geet Mala

Compered with equal finesse in English, when elder
Hamid, suddenly left us, at Bournvita Quiz gala

Most sought after by celebrities and all, leaves huge body
of work as MC and host, the finest in music and sound

*[Context: Reminiscing best voiced Indian RJ, ameen Sayani,
on his demise - end Feb '24]*

§ 11. PANKAJ UDHAS

Another musician and vocalist has been lost by us

Pankaj Udhas always had a smile, did not
at all seem 'udaas' (sad)

His voice had a silky smoothness, apt for 'mai' (drinks) ghazals

'Chitthi'(letter from home) was a chart buster from
another genre, but no hassles

His demeanour was very unassuming, simple, and no fuss

[Context: Simple, silky Indian Ghazal singer passes away - end Feb '24]

§ 12. CHESS PRODIGIES!

Pragganandhaaa (Pragg), Gukesh and Vidit are the
new Indian 'brainees' in chess

In the Candidates Chess Tournament in Toronto,
they are showing their prowess

The winner gets to challenge Ding Liren for
the World Chess Championship

Last year it was Pragg, hopefully, an Indian will
be showcasing that it was not a mere blip

Disruption' is the new buzzword, wherein
newcomers enter, creating a 'nice mess'

[Context: New-age Indian Chess prodigies - mid Apr '24]

§ 13. 'JOSH' of JOS

While Test Cricket, spread over 5 days and two innings
each, is a display of technique

50 overs One-dayer, and 20 overs T20, with an innings each, is
innovation, thinking on feet, physique

Jos Buttler's astuteness and stamina was at full
display over Kolkata IPL team

After fabulous innings by Sunil Narine for KKR, Buttler's 'josh'
made 96 in last 6 overs, chasing 224 in full steam

Shorter versions are exciting for spectators, exacting for
players but are not without critique

*[Context: Jos Butler's finest T20 hurricane innings in Indian
Premier League (IPL) 2024 - mid Apr '24]*

§ 14. CRICKET: ZOOMING AVERAGES

In today's T20, even the high average of 10 runs
per over is becoming a pass

Deep hunger has breached the 14+ average, attempt
is now for 15 or 20 to amass

Batsmen, sorry, Batters have invented and brought
new shots in their armoury

Bowlers too are not far behind with their yorkers and
pace off in their artillery

Pitch 'sizing' and Weather conditions are still the two
imponderables to surpass

[Context: On average runs per over, hitting the roof, in IPL 2024 - mid Apr '24]

§ 15. FABULOUS PLASTICINE ACTORS

Every era unveils actors with plasticine like malleability

They get into the skin of the character with
great finesse and adaptability

Be it Naseer, Shabana, Dustin, Amitabh, Anupam,
Tom, Meryl, Nawaz, Rao, Rekha, Irfan, Jim, to name a few

Simpleton to quirky, vagabond to don, historical to
biographical - on showcase have been all shades and hue

What endears and is left for posterity is their
impactful craft and versatility

*[Context: Some superlative actors who mould themselves
in the character - end Apr '24]*

§ 16. CEREBRAL PALSY RESILIENCE

Cerebral palsy, a congenital and incurable disorder,
affects muscle tone and posture

For the person affected, as well as the caretaker, it
is quite a mental and physical torture

Kudos to 23-year-old Sarika, from Kerala,
with the disease, attempting the Civil Services exam

Hats off to her for her success, with resolve,
resilience, robustness, and a Zen like calm

Shows us all that handicaps can be overcome with
right focus, smile and pleasure

*[Context: On Sarika, affected by cerebral palsy, clearing the
competitive exam through sheer grit - end Apr '24]*

§ 17. FEMALE FATALE, 'QUEER-IS-SHE'

Some new age actresses are not afraid to perform
any hard-hitting meaty role

Bhumi, Radhika, Richa and Swara are not bothered
by the fallout of any troll

There is yet another unconventional actress,
who has displayed great versatility

On the OTT, she has created an unprecedented
furore i.e. Huma, the 'Queer-is-she' (Qureshi)!

Queer as in, unusual, spot-on acting prowess - Politician Queen/
Maharani, and the lovable Home Cook soul

*[Context: A tribute to hard-hitting female Indian actresses,
incl. Huma Qureshi - end Apr '24]*

§ 18. ARCHERS' GLORY!

Jyothi, Aditi, Parneet; and Abhishek, Priyansh, Prathamesh -
unknown names making a mark in the world!

In varied sports, Indians are shining - the above are 3 female and 3
male archers unfurled!

In World Archery Stage 1, in Shanghai, the team won Golds in the
combined female, male and mixed tournaments

Unfortunately, neither talked about much nor headlined are such
fabulous achievements

As Indians, to motivate our citizens, our rejoicing should be
boisterous and open, not muted and knurled

*[Context: On WoMen/Mix Teams glories in
World Archery Championships - early May '24]*

§ 19. YOUNG INDIA'S MOUNTAINEERING TALENT

No accolades are enough for the 16-year-old Ms Kaamya
Karthikeyan becoming the youngest Indian scaling Mt. Everest

Having scaled six highest peaks in six continents, she aims for the
Seven Summits Challenge, by doing the rest

And would become the youngest girl in the world to complete the
challenge, after scaling Antarctica's Mt. Vinson Massif

Product of Navy School, Mumbai, all Indians are proud of her
for the Himalayan climb massive

Post reaching the seventh, she will not only be a girl child icon and
motif but also the world's first and best

[Context: On Kaamya scaling Mt. Everest, en route to accomplishing Seven Summits Challenge - end May '24]

§ 20. INDIAN GLORY AT CANNES 2024

Another glass ceiling broken; another bastion conquered by an Indian

Humongous Congratulations to Payal Kapadia for winning
on her debut feature direction!

As, 'All that we imagine as light' gets the coveted Cannes 2024,
2nd highest Grand Prix Award

Another history in making, kudos to Anasuya Sengupta,
who also won in 'The Shameless', the Best Performance card

After 30 years, and first Indian lady's film featured in the
competition, was itself a fabulous recognition

[Context: Grand Prix win by Indians at Cannes 2024 - end May '24]

§ 21. INDIAN PREMIER LEAGUE 2024

IPL 2024 concludes and whilst the game wins, there
is a deserved third time winner

Kudos to the entire team but more so to Shreyas,
Sunil, Mitchell, Gautam, and franchise KKR?

In consistency, constancy, the commonality is the
owners, their support and Gauti or GG

First two as Captain and now as Mentor, this Delhi
boy has shown his skills, acumen and strategy

Besides political alignment with BCCI, for Team
India's Head Coach, he is the No.1 contender

[Context: KKR's 3rd IPL Trophy, and Gautam Gambhir's association - end May '24]

THEME 8

SUPREME(LY) RATIONAL COURT

§ 1. CONVERTING STATE TO UT

The Judgement's been declared, skims the
surface and is quite muted

Possibly, as any further would have been rather
uncomfortable, disliked and unsuited

Giving a UT (Union Territory), Statehood enables
people more representation

Reversing the same, unilaterally, is a kind of
rights deprivation and dilution

In future, this could have dangerous repercussions, deep-rooted

*[Context: On Kashmir being declared a Union Territory
from a State - mid Dec '23]*

§ 2. GUTSY SC

Fulsome plaudits to SC for gutsy action reversing own judgment

Which had not even been worth its writing on the paper parchment

Setting free, remitting life-sentence of 11 gang
rapists of pregnant Bilkis bibi

Rapists, in connivance with their 'power'ful
connections had made law, a mockery

And were celebrated on release as if they had been innocent

*[Context: Reversal by SC of its own judgement on acquittal of
11 gang rapists of Bilkis Bano - mid Jan '24]*

§ 3. OVERTURNED BUT LATE

Electoral Bonds: Continuing 'Contemprick'
from acouple of months ago

5-bench gutsy SC declares the bonds 'unconstitutional', in one flow

Opacity and Quid Pro Quo: two major reasons,
SC asks for donor details on website

Voters' RTI (Right to Information) sacrificed by
anonymity, requires oversight

Likely challenge aside, ruling coming late, close
to elections, impact may be near zero

[Context: On Electoral Bonds being declared unconstitutional by SC - mid Feb '24]

§ 4. BLATANT RIGGING

Has the conscience been killed or 'protection'
made one so audacious?

Rigging is perpetrated in front of camera, in
mayoral elections, making results fallacious

By the Returning officer, intentionally making
marks on ballots, so they get invalidated

With not an iota of fear, tipping the results in
favour of those not mandated

Supreme Court had to get involved, who castigated it as
"murder of democracy" - so obnoxious!

*[Context: SC judgement on the rigged mayoral elections of
Chandigarh - end Feb '24]*

§ 5. FALI NARIMAN

Sadly, the tallest constitutional law expert passes
away today, at a ripe 95

Fali Nariman was not 95 years old but razor sharp 95 years agile

Nani Palkhiwala, Soli Sorabjee, Fali Nariman had more
than one thing in common

Yes, they were all Parsis but also the finest minds in their profession

FN's esteem: appointed Solicitor General, next day
resigned on Emergency declaration, but still
powers-that-be sought his advice

[Context: On Fali Nariman's demise - end Feb '24]

§ 6. NECESSARY OVERSIGHT

In India, in everything, courts seem to be getting
forcibly involved and embroiled

For keeping the country running justly, and
justifiably keeping government machinery oiled

Be it pollution, enviro-ecology, religion, demolition
or other grey areas, like abortion,

Euthanasia, governance, influence, elections,
gay matters or adoption

Judiciary's oversight is sadly necessary amidst other
governing arms getting soiled and spoiled

[Context: Courts, esp. SC having to get involved and pass judgements on multifarious legislative/administrative issues - early Mar '24]

§ 7. MISDEEDS IN PARLIAMENT

Supreme Court of India surprises yet again and gives another historic judgement

Displaying ample grit and courage to reverse, many years old, own pronouncement

Rape, murder, bribery, call for insurrection (US, are you listening?)..., should get no immunity

Should all humans not be treated equally, in such crimes, to get the same justice and equity?

Even if they are Heads of Govt., MPs, MLAs or committing such deeds in Parliament!

[Context: SC reversing its own judgement on bribery in Parliament not covered by immunity - early Mar '24]

§ 8. ROLE EXPANSION BEING 'GIVEN' TO SC

Does it behove well when SC has to delve into parliamentary issues?

Laws framed by brute majority, executive's own interpretation, media's TRP based reporting - SC has to but step into their shoes

Like ED's delays, Guv's/LG's procrastination, Pollution/Green cover reduction, SBI's reluctance, EBs' validity

Govt's extensions/delays in filling bureaucracy/nonpartisan EC/ judges' vacancies, Speakers' rulings' absurdity

Seems collegium selected SC forum is the only fair check, which dwells and chews

[Context: SC having to get involved and pronounce judgements on virtually many controversial legislative/administrative actions - end Mar '24]

§ 9. JUDICIARY, THE THIRD PILLAR OF DEMOCRACY

Currently, only one institution seems to be mostly
uninfluenced or impartial

And that is the third pillar of democracy, the
Supreme Court which is judiciary's pinnacle

Like in any other organisation, direction, ethics,
sentiments cascade from top downwards

Independently dealing on merit, especially in
judiciary, should likewise percolate upwards

Most institutions under pressure and compromised,
current CJI is the only beacon in the tunnel

[Context: CJI Chandrachud standing his ground on many anti-establishment matters - early Apr '24}

§ 10. BAIL OR JAIL

'Twas a tight-rope walk for the SC considering Delhi CM's bail

Both sides had valid arguments with equally weighted logic trail

The situation was definitely unique and did
smack of timing machinations

Which probably tilted the scales in CM's favour for
interim bail but with limitations

SC ruling clearly stating that it was a rare exception,
providing 15 days relief from jail

[Context: Bail given to Delhi CM, while case being argued, during elections - mid May '24]

§ 11. 'ARREST' ING REASON: A FUNDAMENTAL RIGHT

SC comes in yet again to explain a provision of law, indirectly
assisting the 4th estate i.e. media

NewsClicks founder/editor was taken into custody for doubtful
funding under stringent UAPA (unlawful activities) criteria

He was taken into remand in Oct last without being
given any grounds of arrest

With no relief from HC, it became the raison d'etre
for escalating issue to SC, to contest

Which ordered his release since his Fundamental
Right had been compromised, creating a phobia

*[Context: SC's ruling that the reason for arrest is a
Fundamental Right - end May '24]*

THEME 9

(UN)PHILOSOPHICALLY PONDERED

§ 1. ON TURNING 65!

Now, when I've turned sixty-five
In life's ocean I've but taken a dive
People think I've grown so old
Even water in beer mug, they give me to hold
But amidst noise and chatter, there's still some vibe

[Context: Funny 65! - mid Oct '23]

§ 2. EMOTIONS FOR CHILDREN

A Father (Parent) loves his children, especially first born,
be it a daughter or son
Always, and more so, if it is a special occasion
Be it an anniversary, birthday or festival
Seeing them grow is always a marvel
Possibly, a bad father looks for death as his only redemption

[Context: Father's selfless love and self-deprecation - mid Oct '23]

§ 3. PROGENY FAQs

All children are loved and equally precious for a parent

'Tis true, blood parents or children have absolutely
no substitute or variant

Like every wheel of a vehicle, each child's
relationship and wellbeing matters

Other progeny shouldn't feel upset if even one of
them throws parents' psyche in tatters

This truism has been in the past and is a natural
parental bonding in the current

*[Context: A Father explaining and consoling his
other child/ren - mid Oct '23]*

§ 4. ACRONYMS

Holy smoke! - Name Tina has been overtaken by TINA acronym

After thought, Nota Bene (N.B.) has also got
overshadowed by the NOTA hymn

There Is No Alternative (TINA) to the present vocabulary

Whilst None Of The Above (NOTA) is part of the
new colloquial constabulary

Language is truly becoming an abbreviated calisthenics gym

[Context: The abbreviated language - mid Nov '23]

§ 5. SOME DO'S AND DON'T'S

Do not be fretful in the first conversations of the morning
Don't complain or be spiteful to a person immediately on meeting
Do thank the Creator, for the day gone by, just before going to sleep
Do thank again and seek blessings, on waking up, in thoughts deep
The above takes humongous effort, hats off for actually practicing

[Context: Some philosophical Do's and Don'ts - end Dec '23]

§ 6. KARMA

Keeping no expectations for your deeds, as
per Karma, is a bit of a conundrum

While mundane people 'expect' results, even
gurus preach, 'expecting' people to listen

Karma philosophy can be practiced truly only
with complete detachment

'Cos Eating has an expectation, Meditating has a 'moksh'
culmination, Living has an attachment

Contrarians say, Keeping no expectations is
much like travelling without a destination

[Context: The theory of 'Karma' re-visited - end Dec '23]

§ 7. NEW YEAR RESOLUTIONS

Are New Year Resolutions, Resolute enough

Or are Confabulations, a lot of Confused fluff

Tribulations are Trials one faces in life

Postulations are Possibilities with a lot of hype

Formulations are Formulae to life's successful surf

[Context: New Year Resolutions Philosophised – early Jan '24]

§ 8. HAPPY NEW YEAR 2024

Another year gone by, 2023 has made way for a New 2024

As time flies, we will soon have 2025, the
centurial quarter knocking the door

Have we just grown a year older or matured like wine?

Onus is on us, review the past, face new challenges and shine

Be Rizz, Sponge up new info, Fertile mind is akin
to soft & sweet petrichor

[Context: On New Year Challenges - 01012024]

§ 9. CHANGING FROM OLD TO NEW

Like any other adjacent months, Dec and Jan are
two months side by side

However, the joy and enthusiasm are unlike any
other, difficult to hide

While Dec is full of reverie and introspections

Jan is full of hope and lofty resolutions

Some get zealously fulfilled, others face challenges in their stride

[Context: Dec & Jan juxtaposed - early Jan '24]

§ 10. LGBTQ+

LGBTQ+ is a bit of a tongue twister and a needless enigma

When a person's nature is by Mother Nature, why the stigma?

The only issue which is quite flummoxing and unfathomable

Is when they say, gender feelings change
hourly/daily, actioning which is quite impractical

Making it more challenging to remove this old societal dogma

*[Context: On the challenging, constantly changing
feelings of LGBTQ+ community - early Jan '24]*

§ 11. PRINT MEDIA

A Newspaper is not simply NEWS (of north, east, west, south)
in a paper to be viewed

It contains IDEA (info, details, editorial, articles)
in a SPACE (sports, philosophy, adverts, classifieds,
entertainment) to be mentally chewed

Longevity, art of writing, language ethics are its forte

Where audio, video, social and other media do not foray

It's a medium in which all is concisely sewed and glued

[Context: A thought on What's a Newspaper? - early Jan '24]

§ 12. LOVE & FAITH

Don't let crush, rush or trust, rust

Love & Faith in friendship are a must

These are the best foundations and definitely amongst the first

Otherwise, the ballooning relationship pricks and gets burst

For a healthy bonding score, core is as crucial as the crust

[Context: A thought on Friendship's Love & Faith - early Jan '24]

§ 13. HARD CHOICES

Greek mythology coined the idiom
'between Scylla and Charybdis'
Meaning selecting an option from two tough choices
Then came, 'between the Devil and deep blue sea'
Followed by the era of 'between a rock and a
hard place', you see!
All conveying the same sense of 'choosing
the lesser evil' in different voices

[Context: 'Hard Choices' of different eras - mid Jan '24]

§ 14. FRIENDSHIP

Two friends are similar to a railway track pair
Supporting each other and showing their care
Running side by side, giving strength to each other
Being together in all climes without a bother
Sharing all loads and challenges without a scare

[Context: Friendship simile - what ought to be but may not be - mid Jan '24]

§ 15. OUTSTANDING PASSION STANDS OUT

Hospitality is the business of a hotelier
Creativity develops wings in an atelier
Whatever be one's passion
Trait, understanding has to be the traction
For standing out, one's got to be an outlier

[Context: True Passion defined - mid Jan '24]

§ 16. EXTRAORDINARY!

Famous are never the regular fare
They are always extraordinaire
Be it animals, fish, birds or humans
Extra spark, uniqueness marks the difference
Such have to be handled with utmost care

[Context: Handling extraordinary ones - mid Jan '24]

§ 17. RELIGION'S A PERSONAL BELIEF SYSTEM

Religion is Personal Faith, not to be worn on the sleeve
More so, if one is in the business of hide and deceive
Political leadership is not for the faint-hearted
Where facts are hidden, lies peddled unwarranted
Ole' man sayeth, by such actions, 'moksha' will
be difficult to achieve

[Context: My strong belief -- Religion and Politics should never be mixed -- mid Jan '24]

§ 18. THE YO-YO LIFE

In yesteryears, 'twas said, Life's full of thorns and roses
Amidst today's health fads, either it is bland or replete with spices
Ups and downs are part of the journey
Like wins and losses in any sports tourney
In this maddening world, man is tackling not daily but hourly crisis

[Context: The Ups & Downs in life, re-articulated - mid Jan '24]

§ 19. MAKING MISTAKE IS HUMAN

For humans, making a mistake may carry
some guilt but is not a shame

'Pandit' Nehru, after the '62 Chinese incursion
owned up and felt the same

After the '75 Emergency, calling for elections
in '77 showed repentance

It takes a large heart and humility for owning a
mistake and acceptance

Sadly, today's egotist leaders feel they are gods, and
play only the blame game

*[Context: Politicians owning up a mistake is a rarity -
the greater the persona & ego, the rarer the acceptance - end Jan '24]*

§ 20. DEATH IMPACT

Death, when it comes and under which circumstances,
impacts different people differently

To both the person who died and the those left
behind, be it friends or family

Whilst Sudden and/or Untimely deaths are
painful for those who are still living;

Protracted illness prepares all, and death is
deliverance to those dead, from suffering

Death grief causes outbursts in some, others
break internally, keeping silent facade stoically

[Context: Sudden and Slow Death visualised - mid Feb '24]

§ 21. CUISINES

'Tis said that there are only three basic cuisines
in this entire world

Rest are all variations, with the three in the core curled

Continentals come from the French, conjuring up magic,
baking with flour, eggs, meat and cheese

Orientals with hotpot, seafood, meat and tongue
twirling noodles are shown the way by the Chinese

Spices, Veggies, Curries in the wok are a boon from the
Indians, satiating taste buds, keeping the senses swirled

[Context: 3 Leading cuisines simply defined - mid Feb '24]

§ 22. GANDHIANISM RE-EXPLAINED

Winning all by Love, Tolerance, Non-violence are
considered 3 foremost Gandhian tenets

People mistake them as Absolute, however,
each one has own threshold limits

Otherwise, Gandhiji would have 'tolerated'
hindu-muslim riots, and white racism

Halting govt. machinery, peaceful protests sans
effective weapons seem Non-violence pragmatism

Winning ALL by love is also not absolute: Jinnah
and Godse are some tipping point exhibits

*[Context: Commenting on Shiv Khera's Gandhian assessment
going viral - mid Feb '24]*

§ 23. GRAMMATICAL SYMBOLS

(! Exclamation is a Wow! (? Question mark is a How? and (:
Colon is two rump dots where details append

(; Semi colon separates, while (?! Interrobang is a
unique two-tone emotional bend

(') Apostrophe shortens - 'tis a writing atrophy,
while doubling (" ") Inverted commas/Quotation
marks is a chatter

(-) Hyphen is a small hiccup joint, whilst a (--) Dash dashingly
dashes away matter

Finally, (,) Comma is a comatose pause, before
(.) Full stop brings The End

[Context: A symbolic play with grammatical symbols - mid Mar '24]

§ 24. MONTHS' SERENADING TO THEIR OWNTUNES

Kicking off 'Jaan'query is why is there dual pronunciation
only for February (Febuary)?

'March'ing along, A-prill May encounter some
soil absorption worry

So, our Jun-ior experiments, Julie(nnes) are cut,
for the August agri-experts' gathering

Where 'Come September' serenades the
musical Octo-bar metering

Nova-'ember' of stubble pollutes, leading to
DeCe (Distt Court/Collector) mber's entry

[Context: Months, in their yearly dance – mid Mar '24]

§ 25. INSURANCE VS ASSURANCE

In risk cover terminology, there is insurance,
and there is assurance

This confuses people as they do not know the difference

Insurance is when the covered incident,
like fire/burglary/floods, may or may not happen

Assurance is when an incident will definitely happen,
like death, but timing is uncertain

Risk cover is required for both - to get compensation
for a re-boot or leave the family with monetary subsistence

*[Context: An educative clarification about Insurance
and assurance, which most are unaware of - end Mar '24]*

§ 26. TOUGHNESS

Being arrogant and gruff

Does not make a person tough

Having strength with mental and ethical humility,

And not a cynosure but simplicity

Is what defines toughness, the real stuff

[Context: Political leaders talking tough - early Apr '24]

§ 27. INCOMMUNICADO

At times, one feels life is useless and not worth living

Especially, if your loved one totally stops communicating

Am I to blame or is his mind weak?

Even if I am to blame, is the solution 'no speak'?

I weep silently, pray fervently but alas, nothing's improving

[Context: A friend's/son's hurtful break in communications - early Apr '24]

§ 28. RELATIONSHIPS

Many a times, I ponder, if there is indeed any
relationship that is sustainable

The one with friends is mostly selfish, off and on, and not stable

Birth and even blood relationships break heart,
get scattered over time

What one is left with is only oneself, which is the only, truly 'mine'

The lonely self wants to return to The Creator,
the only relationship cherishable!

*[Context: Philosophical meanderings - the only sustainable
relationship seems to be with The Creator - early Apr '24]*

§ 29. LIFE!!!

What is ***LIFE*** - is it: ***L*** ousy or ***L*** ovely?
I conic or wasted in ***I*** gnominy?
F ulsome or deeply ***F*** rustrating?
E nnui ridden or ***E*** nticing?
Whatever it is - forever it remains a Solitary Journey!

[Context: Life Simply Defined – mid Apr '24]

§ 30. COMPETITIVE ATTEMPTS - WHEN IS ENOUGH?

Competitive exams, especially Pan-India ones
are indeed quite tough

But normally three attempts
(not going up to twelve years), should be enough

Maybe for special categories, the attempts
could be extended to five

Unsuccessful thereafter, choose a second
calling timely, not waste life

The longer it gets, despondency, depression results
in some even taking their lives in a huff

[Context: On someone passing a competitive exam in his 12th attempt - is it worth it? - mid Apr '24]

§ 31. TINY MOSQUITO, HIGH IQ!

The tiny mosquito, has become audacious and
evolved over the years

Now, with thread like thinness, it squeezes thru
the smallest mesh, and at us, it jeers

Momentary racquet stunning, higher temperature and
wind power threshold, it's stronger body copiously procreates

With 360° sight, it scoots with any motion, and the blue
light fatal attraction, it mockingly avoids and navigates

Displaying higher evolved IQ, it merrily sucks blood
silently, without a buzz in the ears

[Context: Tiny Mosquito, Mighty sting - end Apr '24]

§ 32. UNBRIDLED POWER'S CONS

With leaders across wanting to cling to unbridled power

Day by day, politics, world over, is stooping lower and getting dirtier

No one is certain whether to believe the official story

Or whether the truth is the one touted as the conspiracy theory

Be it Israel-Hamas, Russia-Ukraine, number of Balakot deaths,
Sandeshkhali rape - issues are getting murkier and messier

*[Context: Lok Sabha elections campaigning, and scenarios prevalent
across the world - early May '24]*

§ 33. HUMAN TRUST EROSION

On hearing such news, one wonders what is
happening to people and this world?

GP, who treated philanthropically too, Dr Paul's
life was snuffed out and lulled

By no less than a 65 year old maid, who had
been working for the doctor couple for 24 years

Faith in humans and humanity goes for a toss, when such
instances come to the ears

Loyalty and long association lose their sense of comfort, when
such incidents get unfurled

*[Context: Dr Paul's murder in Jangpura, Delhi by a 24
years association, 65 years old maid - mid May '24]*

§ 34. LIVE AND LET LIVE!

Dhabolkar's 11 year old murder case, so prolonged, is both
perplexing and intriguing

The alleged kingpin, Tawde, was acquitted while
some others are jail-a-rotting

However, the modus operandi is the most
disturbing of all the matters

Dhabolkar was a superstition fighter whereas the
murderers are 'sanaatan hindu' believers

Superstition exists in all religions - ideology to each his own,
shouldn't be reason for the dastardly killing

*[Context: Shameful reason for taking human life due to
different beliefs - mid May '24]*

§ 35. NEWSPAPER DETOX

'Devil is in the details', and 'A wholesome package' is why newspaper is valued even today, by many

Quick browsing on various social media platforms, provides info, albeit perfunctory, for just a penny

Multiple handles and fora, fast changing tech, ambitious lifestyle had made life so 'rushed' for Gen Z

That being overtaken by Gen Alpha and soon Gen Beta, amidst today's frenetic pace, has not come easy

Now, they appreciate better, the detox impact of the dailies, leaving them with feelings uncanny

[Context: Response to Times of India's POV (Point of View) on newspaper reading - mid May '24]

§ 36. SELFISH & SHAMELESS LOVE

Protecting a child even when he drinks, drives, and drives a young couple to death, is not true parenting

What was the fault in the parenting of the couples' parents, who lost their children lamenting

True parenting, in such situations, needs to be empathetic, remorseful, selfless, not selfish

Saving own child through bribery, when his inebriated driving caused deaths so gory and foolish

Blaming driver, pulling strings, swapping blood samples reeks of parents being self-centred and unrepenting

[Context: POV comment to TOI's Pune Techie couple 'murder' in Porche road accident - end May '24]

§ 37. SAY NO TO TOBACCO

31st May is designated as World NO Tobacco Day

Grow for medicine but don't chew, snuff, smoke or play

Enough evidence, tobacco causes cancer

De-addict from the known devil's possible ulcer

Not worth risking for such ephemeral pleasures,
just say "No Way!"

*[Context: Rumination about Tobacco on
World NO Tobacco Day - 31052024]*

§ 38. WORLD MILK DAY

1st June: World Milk Day! - the very first nutrient
of a newborn, which the world celebrates

Today, there are many kinds - soy, almond,
camel, cow and from other ungulates

Milk is considered as only one of its ilk i.e. most
complete food by Mother Nature!

Especially for the poor, amongst all foods, it carries
the tag of importance and highest stature

But 'To Milk or Not to Milk', the Vegan differs,
calls it 'snatching' and denigrates

[Context: Inner dialogue on World Milk Day - 01062024]